## Contents

## 21<sup>st</sup> Century

1) Who scored Sunderland's first goal of the 21<sup>st</sup> Century?

2) Who was the manager of Sunderland at the beginning of the 21<sup>st</sup> Century?

3) Who did Ellis Short replace as chairman in 2011?

4) How many goals did Kevin Phillips score in the 1999/2000 season to secure the Premiership Golden Boot award?

5) How many games did Paolo Di Canio manage Sunderland for?

6) How many points did Sunderland win during the 2005/06 Premier League season in which they finished bottom of the table?

7) Who was the clubs' top league goal scorer, with 13 goals, when they won promotion to the Premier League in the 2006/07 season?

8) Who became the first Romanian to represent Sunderland after he was signed in 2014?

9) Which former Black Cats player scored during the 2-1 loss to Burton in April 2018 which saw Sunderland relegated to League One?

10) What squad number did John O'Shea wear throughout his time at the club?

11) Which former Sunderland player came on as a substitute for Charlton during the League One Play-Off Final in 2019?

12) How many points did Sunderland win when claiming the Championship title in the 2004/05 season?

13) Against which team did Jordan Henderson come on as a substitute to make his debut for Sunderland?

14) Who replaced Gustavo Poyet as manager in March 2015?

15) Darren Bent scored a hat trick against which team in a 4-0 home win in March 2010?

16) Which Sunderland player volleyed in a spectacular own goal during the 8-0 loss at Southampton in October 2014?

17) Who took over the club captaincy from Gary Breen in 2006?

18) Which Sunderland player scored two own goals in the first half of Sunderland's 3-1 home loss to Charlton in February 2003?

19) During 2012 which Sunderland striker won his only England cap in a friendly against the Netherlands?

20) What was the result in Sam Allardyce's last game in charge?

21) Darren Bent famously scored via a deflection off a beach ball in the match against Liverpool in 2009, but what was the final score of the game?

22) Sunderland had a match abandoned due to snow after 20 minutes against which opposition in April 2006?

23) Which Sunderland player was shortlisted for the PFA Young Player of the Year award in 2017?

24) What was the result in Phil Parkinson's first game as Sunderland manager?

## Transfers I

1) Which player arrived from Argentinos Juniors in July 2000?

2) Sunderland signed which defender from Chelsea in August 2000?

3) Which former Arsenal defender was released by Sunderland in September 2000?

4) From which club was Jason McAteer bought in October 2001?

5) Who was Alex Rae sold to in September 2001?

6) Phil Babb arrived from which Portuguese club in July 2002?

7) Which goalkeeper was signed from Derby County in January 2003?

8) Dean Whitehead was bought from which club in June 2004?

9) Sunderland signed which player on a free from Newcastle in June 2004?

10) Kevin Phillips was sold to which team in August 2003?

11) Which side did Michael Gray sign for after leaving in January 2004?

12) Which experienced striker signed on a free from Leeds United in March 2005?

13) Sunderland bought which goalkeeper from Ipswich Town in June 2005?

14) Rory Delap was signed from which club in January 2006?

15) Sean Thornton was sold in July 2005 to which side?

16) Which two players did Sunderland buy from Wigan Athletic in August 2006?

17) Which club was Jon Stead sold to in January 2007?

18) Which former Newcastle player was bought from Cardiff City in July 2007?

19) Ian Harte signed in the summer of 2007 from which Spanish side?

20) Sunderland signed three players from Tottenham in the summer of 2008, who were they?

21) Lorik Cana arrived from which French club in July 2009?

22) Which midfielder was bought from Wigan in August 2009?

23) Who was Grant Leadbitter sold to in September 2009?

**First Goals I** – Name the clubs that these players scored their first goal for the club against

1) Jordan Henderson

2) Claudio Reyna

3) Tore Andre Flo

4) Marcus Stewart

5) Jeff Whitley

6) Aiden McGeady

7) Stephane Sessegnon

8) Daryl Murphy

9) Dwight Yorke

10) Lamine Kone

11) Johnny Williams

12) Wahbi Khazri

13) Andy Reid

14) Jermain Defoe

## Red Cards

1) Which goalkeeper was sent off in the Championship defeat to QPR in March 2018?

2) In the 2013/14 Premier League season Wes Brown was sent off three times, can you name the three teams he was dismissed against?

3) Who was controversially sent off in the 3-0 loss to Manchester United in April 2017?

4) John Oster was sent off for two yellow card offenses against which club in February 2001?

5) Who was sent off after receiving two yellow cards in the 1-0 home loss to Liverpool in January 2015?

6) Sunderland went on to beat Bournemouth 2-1 away from home in November 2016 despite which player being sent off with the score at 1-1?

7) Who was sent off against Liverpool in a 1-0 defeat at Anfield in August 2005?

8) Which defender was given two yellow cards in the loss to Norwich City in March 2014?

9) Who was sent off in the 4-0 loss to Cardiff City in Division One in February 2004?

10) Which two players were sent off for Sunderland in the 1-0 away defeat to Hull City in November 2013?

11) Which Sunderland player was sent off late on in the 1-0 Wear-Tyne derby defeat at the Stadium of Light in August 2011?

12) Marcus Stewart was dismissed against which team in April 2003?

13) Who was sent off against Portsmouth in the first leg of the League One Play-Off Semi Final in 2019?

14) Who received his second yellow card late on just before Manchester secured a 2-2 draw in the October 2009 game at Old Trafford?

15) Paul McShane was given a straight red in a 3-2 defeat to which team in October 2007?

16) Which two players were sent off in the 3-0 defeat to Peterborough United in the League One meeting between the sides in August 2019?

## Memorable Goals

1) Jermain Defoe scored his remarkable left footed volley past which Newcastle goalkeeper to win the derby in April 2015?

2) Which unlikely player scored a solo goal in the 3-0 away win over Chelsea in November 2010, beating three players before finishing?

3) Boudewijn Zenden scored a brilliant left footed volley against which team in April 2010?

4) Craig Gardner volleyed in from 25 yards to secure a 2-0 win over which team in January 2012?

5) Who produced a sensational scissor kick away at Liverpool in August 2011 in a 1-1 draw?

6) Whabi Khazri scored with a superb volley in the 3-2 victory over Chelsea in May 2016, but who was in goal for the opposition?

7) Fraizer Campbell hit a dipping volley against who in February 2012 in a 3-0 win?

8) Jermain lens produced a sublime chip that went in off the underside of the bar against which team in October 2015?

9) Who scored with a perfect left footed volley from the edge of the box in the January 2006 game away at Fulham?

10) Who rounded off a swift counter attack with a long-range striker to give Sunderland a 3-2 win over Burnley in April 2007?

11) Wahbi Khazri scored direct from a corner during the 2-2 draw with which side in April 2017?

12) Chris Maguire intercepted a pass before scoring a powerful effort from 25 yards against which opposition in October 2018?

## Memorable Games

1) Sunderland sealed their Premier League survival in May 2016 by beating Everton 3-0, who scored a brace that day?

2) Who saved a penalty from Alan Shearer during the 2-1 victory at St James' Park in November 2000?

3) Sunderland raised their hopes of Championship survival by winning 4-1 away from home against which team in March 2018?

4) Which team were defeated 5-0 by Sunderland in League One in October 2019?

5) Who scored a ferocious free kick from the edge of the box to secure a 2-1 Wear-Tyne derby victory at home in October 2008?

6) Sunderland won 5-0 away from home in the Championship against which side in May 2007?

7) Darren Bent scored the only goal of the game with a 90th minute penalty against which side to provide Sunderland's first win of the 2010/11 season?

8) Everton beat Sunderland 7-1 in November 2007, but who scored the only goal for Sunderland?

9) Which Newcastle player was sent off as Sunderland won 3-0 at the Stadium of Light in October 2015?

10) Who scored in injury time to give Sunderland a 1-0 win over Spurs in their first game back in the Premier League in August 2007?

11) Which Newcastle player scored a late own goal to hand Sunderland a 1-1 draw in October 2012?

12) Which Manchester United player scored a late own goal to hand Sunderland a 2-1 win in February 2016?

13) Who was the Sunderland manager when they secured a long-awaited win at St James' Park by winning 3-0 in April 2013?

14) Who scored deep into injury time to give Sunderland a 2-1 win over Charlton on the opening day of the League One season in 2018?

## Transfers II

1) From which French club was Asamoah Gyan purchased in 2010?

2) Darren Bent left the club in January 2011 to join which side?

3) Which two players arrived from Manchester United in July 2011?

4) Who did Anton Ferdinand sign for after leaving Sunderland in August 2011?

5) Which striker arrived from Swansea City in January 2013?

6) Which forward left the club in February 2013 to sign for Motherwell?

7) From which club did Sunderland buy Jozy Altidore in July 2013?

8) Right back Ahmed Elmohamady was sold to which team in June 2013?

9) Which midfield player was brought in from Manchester City in August 2014?

10) Which central midfielder signed for West Brom after leaving Sunderland in July 2014?

11) Jermain Lens arrived in the summer of 2015 from which club?

12) Sunderland signed which player from Bayern Munich in January of 2016?

13) Who did Connor Wickham sign for in August 2015?

14) Which player did Sunderland buy from Chelsea in August 2016?

15) Which team was Emanuele Giaccherini sold to in July 2016?

16) From which club was Aiden McGeady signed in July 2017?

17) Which winger was brought in from Brighton in January 2018?

18) Who was Paddy McNair sold to in June 2018?

19) Luke O'Nien was brought in from which team in July 2018?

20) Will Grigg was signed from which team at the end of the 2019 January transfer window?

21) Josh Maja signed for which French team in the same January transfer window?

22) Which Dutch team did Lee Cattermole sign for from Sunderland in August 2019?

23) Josh Scowen arrived from which club in January 2020?

**Cup Games**

1) Which player missed his penalty as Sunderland lost the Football League Trophy Final to Portsmouth in 2019?

2) Sunderland had knocked the Newcastle Under 23 side out of the competition by what score line?

3) Sunderland lost 1-0 to Millwall in the FA Cup Semi-Finals in 2004, who scored the winning goal?

4) Who scored the winning goal as Sunderland beat Sheffield United 1-0 in the FA Cup Quarter Final of 2004?

5) Which team had Sunderland beaten 1-0 in the FA Cup Third Round in 2004?

6) Who knocked Sunderland out of the FA Cup at the First Round Stage in 2019?

7) Sunderland beat Peterborough away from home in the Third Round of the FA Cup in 2012, what was the final score?

8) Which team beat Sunderland in the FA Cup Third Round of 2018?

9) Sunderland hammered Cambridge United by what score in the League Cup Second Round in 2002?

10) Manchester City beat Sunderland 3-1 in the 2014 League Cup Final, but who had put the Black Cats ahead in the game?

11) Sunderland had knocked Manchester United out at the Semi Final Stage in the 2014 League Cup on penalties, who was in goal for Sunderland in the shoot out?

## First Goals II

1) Duncan Watmore

2) David Healy

3) Josh Maja

4) Fraizer Campbell

5) Ji Dong-Won

6) Bryan Oviedo

7) John O'Shea

8) James Vaughan

9) Steven Fletcher

10) Billy Jones

11) Luke O'Nien

12) Fabio Borini

13) Lynden Gooch

14) Chris Maguire

# Answers

## 21st Century – Answers

1) Who scored Sunderland's first goal of the 21st Century?
**Niall Quinn in a 4-1 loss away to Arsenal**

2) Who was the manager of Sunderland at the beginning of the 21st Century?
**Peter Reid**

3) Who did Ellis Short replace as chairman in 2011?
**Niall Quinn**

4) How many goals did Kevin Phillips score in the 1999/2000 season to secure the Premiership Golden Boot award?
**30**

5) How many games did Paolo Di Canio manage Sunderland for?
**13**

6) How many points did Sunderland win during the 2005/06 Premier League season in which they finished bottom of the table?
**15**

7) Who was the clubs' top league goal scorer, with 13 goals, when they won promotion to the Premier League in the 2006/07 season?
**David Connolly**

8) Who became the first Romanian to represent Sunderland after he was signed in 2014?
**Costel Pantilimon**

9) Which former Black Cats player scored during the 2-1 loss to Burton in April 2018 which saw Sunderland relegated to League One?
**Darren Bent**

10) What squad number did John O'Shea wear throughout his time at the club?
**16**

11) Which former Sunderland player came on as a substitute for Charlton during the League One Play-Off Final in 2019?
**Jonny Williams**

12) How many points did Sunderland win when claiming the Championship title in the 2004/05 season?
**94**

13) Against which team did Jordan Henderson come on as a substitute to make his debut for Sunderland?
**Chelsea**

14) Who replaced Gustavo Poyet as manager in March 2015?
**Dick Advocaat**

15) Darren Bent scored a hat trick against which team in a 4-0 home win in March 2010?
**Bolton Wanderers**

16) Which Sunderland player volleyed in a spectacular own goal during the 8-0 loss at Southampton in October 2014?
**Santiago Vergini**

17) Who took over the club captaincy from Gary Breen in 2006?
**Dean Whitehead**

18) Which Sunderland player scored two own goals in the first half of Sunderland's 3-1 home loss to Charlton in February 2003?
**Michael Proctor**

19) During 2012 which Sunderland striker won his only England cap in a friendly against the Netherlands?
**Fraizer Campbell**

20) What was the result in Sam Allardyce's last game in charge?
**Watford 2-2 Sunderland**

21) Darren Bent famously scored via a deflection off a beach ball in the match against Liverpool in 2009, but what was the final score of the game?
**Sunderland 1-0 Liverpool**

22) Sunderland had a match abandoned due to snow after 20 minutes against which opposition in April 2006?
**Fulham**

23) Which Sunderland player was shortlisted for the PFA Young Player of the Year award in 2017?
**Jordan Pickford**

24) What was the result in Phil Parkinson's first game as Sunderland manager?
**Wycombe 1-0 Sunderland**

## Transfers I – Answers

1) Which player arrived from Argentinos Juniors in July 2000?
**Julio Arca**

2) Sunderland signed which defender from Chelsea in August 2000?
**Emerson Thome**

3) Which former Arsenal defender was released by Sunderland in September 2000?
**Steve Bould**

4) From which club was Jason McAteer bought in October 2001?
**Blackburn Rovers**

5) Who was Alex Rae sold to in September 2001?
**Wolverhampton Wanderers**

6) Phil Babb arrived from which Portuguese club in July 2002?
**Sporting Lisbon**

7) Which goalkeeper was signed from Derby County in January 2003?
**Mart Poom**

8) Dean Whitehead was bought from which club in June 2004?
**Oxford United**

9) Sunderland signed which player on a free from Newcastle in June 2004?
**Steven Caldwell**

10) Kevin Phillips was sold to which team in August 2003?
**Southampton**

11) Which side did Michael Gray sign for after leaving in January 2004?
**Blackburn Rovers**

12) Which experienced striker signed on a free from Leeds United in March 2005?
**Brian Deane**

13) Sunderland bought which goalkeeper from Ipswich Town in June 2005?
**Kelvin Davis**

14) Rory Delap was signed from which club in January 2006?
**Southampton**

15) Sean Thornton was sold in July 2005 to which side?
**Doncaster Rovers**

16) Which two players did Sunderland buy from Wigan Athletic in August 2006?
**David Connolly and Graham Kavanagh**

17) Which club was Jon Stead sold to in January 2007?
**Sheffield United**

18) Which former Newcastle player was bought from Cardiff City in July 2007?
**Michael Chopra**

19) Ian Harte signed in the summer of 2007 from which Spanish side?
**Levante**

20) Sunderland signed three players from Tottenham in the summer of 2008, who were they?
**Teemu Tainio, Pascal Chimbonda and Steed Malbranque**

21) Lorik Cana arrived from which French club in July 2009?
**Marseille**

22) Which midfielder was bought from Wigan in August 2009?
**Lee Cattermole**

23) Who was Grant Leadbitter sold to in September 2009?
**Ipswich Town**

## First Goals I – Answers

1) Jordan Henderson
   **Birmingham City**

2) Claudio Reyna
   **Everton**

3) Tore Andre Flo
   **Manchester United**

4) Marcus Stewart
   **Arsenal**

5) Jeff Whitley
   **West Ham**

6) Aiden McGeady
   **Norwich City**

7) Stephane Sessegnon
   **Wigan Athletic**

8) Daryl Murphy
   **Tottenham Hotspur**

9) Dwight Yorke
   **Stoke City**

10) Lamine Kone
    **Everton**

11) Johnny Williams
    **Middlesbrough**

12) Wahbi Khazri
    **Manchester United**

13) Andy Reid
    **West Ham**

14) Jermain Defoe
    **Burnley**

## Red Cards – Answers

1) Which goalkeeper was sent off in the Championship defeat to QPR in March 2018?
**Jason Steele**

2) In the 2013/14 Premier League season Wes Brown was sent off three times, can you name the three teams he was dismissed against?
**Stoke City, Norwich City and Hull City**

3) Who was controversially sent off in the 3-0 loss to Manchester United in April 2017?
**Seb Larsson**

4) John Oster was sent off for two yellow card offenses against which club in February 2001?
**Leicester City**

5) Who was sent off after receiving two yellow cards in the 1-0 home loss to Liverpool in January 2015?
**Liam Bridcutt**

6) Sunderland went on to beat Bournemouth 2-1 away from home in November 2016 despite which player being sent off with the score at 1-1?
**Steven Pienaar**

7) Who was sent off against Liverpool in a 1-0 defeat at Anfield in August 2005?
**Andrew Welsh**

8) Which defender was given two yellow cards in the loss to Norwich City in March 2014?
**Marcos Alonso**

9) Who was sent off in the 4-0 loss to Cardiff City in Division One in February 2004?
**Joachim Bjorklund**

10) Which two players were sent off for Sunderland in the 1-0 away defeat to Hull City in November 2013?
**Andrea Dossena and Lee Cattermole**

11) Which Sunderland player was sent off late on in the 1-0 Wear-Tyne derby defeat at the Stadium of Light in August 2011?
**Phil Bardsley**

12) Marcus Stewart was dismissed against which team in April 2003?
**Birmingham City**

13) Who was sent off against Portsmouth in the first leg of the League One Play-Off Semi Final in 2019?
**Alim Ozturk**

14) Who received his second yellow card late on just before Manchester secured a 2-2 draw in the October 2009 game at Old Trafford?
**Kieran Richardson**

15) Paul McShane was given a straight red in a 3-2 defeat to which team in October 2007?

**Arsenal**

16) Which two players were sent off in the 3-0 defeat to Peterborough United in the League One meeting between the sides in August 2019?

**Luke O'Nien and Charlie Wyke**

## Memorable Goals – Answers

1) Jermain Defoe scored his remarkable left footed volley past which Newcastle goalkeeper to win the derby in April 2015?
**Tim Krul**

2) Which unlikely player scored a solo goal in the 3-0 away win over Chelsea in November 2010, beating three players before finishing?
**Nedum Onuoha**

3) Boudewijn Zenden scored a brilliant left footed volley against which team in April 2010?
**Tottenham Hotspur**

4) Craig Gardner volleyed in from 25 yards to secure a 2-0 win over which team in January 2012?
**Swansea City**

5) Who produced a sensational scissor kick away at Liverpool in August 2011 in a 1-1 draw?
**Seb Larsson**

6) Whabi Khazri scored with a superb volley in the 3-2 victory over Chelsea in May 2016, but who was in goal for the opposition?
**Thibaut Courtois**

7) Fraizer Campbell hit a dipping volley against who in February 2012 in a 3-0 win?
**Norwich City**

8) Jermain lens produced a sublime chip that went in off the underside of the bar against which team in October 2015?
**West Ham**

9) Who scored with a perfect left footed volley from the edge of the box in the January 2006 game away at Fulham?
**Liam Lawrence**

10) Who rounded off a swift counter attack with a long-range striker to give Sunderland a 3-2 win over Burnley in April 2007?
**Carlos Edwards**

11) Wahbi Khazri scored direct from a corner during the 2-2 draw with which side in April 2017?
**West Ham**

12) Chris Maguire intercepted a pass before scoring a powerful effort from 25 yards against which opposition in October 2018?
**Southend**

## Memorable Games – Answers

1) Sunderland sealed their Premier League survival in May 2016 by beating Everton 3-0, who scored a brace that day?
**Lamine Kone**

2) Who saved a penalty from Alan Shearer during the 2-1 victory at St James' Park in November 2000?
**Thomas Sorensen**

3) Sunderland raised their hopes of Championship survival by winning 4-1 away from home against which team in March 2018?
**Derby County**

4) Which team were defeated 5-0 by Sunderland in League One in October 2019?
**Tranmere Rovers**

5) Who scored a ferocious free kick from the edge of the box to secure a 2-1 Wear-Tyne derby victory at home in October 2008?
**Kieran Richardson**

6) Sunderland won 5-0 away from home in the Championship against which side in May 2007?
**Luton Town**

7) Darren Bent scored the only goal of the game with a 90th minute penalty against which side to provide Sunderland's first win of the 2010/11 season?
**Manchester City**

8) Everton beat Sunderland 7-1 in November 2007, but who scored the only goal for Sunderland?
**Dwight Yorke**

9) Which Newcastle player was sent off as Sunderland won 3-0 at the Stadium of Light in October 2015?
**Fabricio Coloccini**

10) Who scored in injury time to give Sunderland a 1-0 win over Spurs in their first game back in the Premier League in August 2007?
**Michael Chopra**

11) Which Newcastle player scored a late own goal to hand Sunderland a 1-1 draw in October 2012?
**Demba Ba**

12) Which Manchester United player scored a late own goal to hand Sunderland a 2-1 win in February 2016?
**David De Gea**

13) Who was the Sunderland manager when they secured a long-awaited win at St James' Park by winning 3-0 in April 2013?
**Paulo Di Canio**

14) Who scored deep into injury time to give Sunderland a 2-1 win over Charlton on the opening day of the League One season in 2018?
**Lynden Gooch**

## Transfers II – Answers

1) From which French club was Asamoah Gyan purchased in 2010?
**Rennes**

2) Darren Bent left the club in January 2011 to join which side?
**Aston Villa**

3) Which two players arrived from Manchester United in July 2011?
**Wes Brown and John O'Shea**

4) Who did Anton Ferdinand sign for after leaving Sunderland in August 2011?
**QPR**

5) Which striker arrived from Swansea City in January 2013?
**Danny Graham**

6) Which forward left the club in February 2013 to sign for Motherwell?
**James McFadden**

7) From which club did Sunderland buy Jozy Altidore in July 2013?
**AZ Alkmaar**

8) Right back Ahmed Elmohamady was sold to which team in June 2013?
**Hull City**

9) Which midfield player was brought in from Manchester City in August 2014?
**Jack Rodwell**

10) Which central midfielder signed for West Brom after leaving Sunderland in July 2014?
**Craig Gardner**

11) Jermain Lens arrived in the summer of 2015 from which club?
**Dynamo Kiev**

12) Sunderland signed which player from Bayern Munich in January of 2016?
**Jan Kirchhoff**

13) Who did Connor Wickham sign for in August 2015?
**Crystal Palace**

14) Which player did Sunderland buy from Chelsea in August 2016?
**Papy Djilobodji**

15) Which team was Emanuele Giaccherini sold to in July 2016?
**Napoli**

16) From which club was Aiden McGeady signed in July 2017?
**Everton**

17) Which winger was brought in from Brighton in January 2018?
**Kazenga Lua Lua**

18) Who was Paddy McNair sold to in June 2018?
**Middlesbrough**

19) Luke O'Nien was brought in from which team in July 2018?
**Wycombe**

20) Will Grigg was signed from which team at the end of the 2019 January transfer window?
**Wigan Athletic**

21) Josh Maja signed for which French team in the same January transfer window?
**Bordeaux**

22) Which Dutch team did Lee Cattermole sign for from Sunderland in August 2019?
**VVV Venlo**

23) Josh Scowen arrived from which club in January 2020?
**QPR**

## Cup Games – Answers

1) Which player missed his penalty as Sunderland lost the Football League Trophy Final to Portsmouth in 2019?
**Lee Cattermole**

2) Sunderland had knocked the Newcastle Under 23 side out of the competition by what score line?
**4-0**

3) Sunderland lost 1-0 to Millwall in the FA Cup Semi-Finals in 2004, who scored the winning goal?
**Tim Cahill**

4) Who scored the winning goal as Sunderland beat Sheffield United 1-0 in the FA Cup Quarter Final of 2004?
**Tommy Smith**

5) Which team had Sunderland beaten 1-0 in the FA Cup Third Round in 2004?
**Hartlepool**

6) Who knocked Sunderland out of the FA Cup at the First Round Stage in 2019?
**Gillingham**

7) Sunderland beat Peterborough away from home in the Third Round of the FA Cup in 2012, what was the final score?
**Peterborough 0-2 Sunderland**

8) Which team beat Sunderland in the FA Cup Third Round of 2018?
**Middlesbrough**

9) Sunderland hammered Cambridge United by what score in the League Cup Second Round in 2002?
**7-0**

10) Manchester City beat Sunderland 3-1 in the 2014 League Cup Final, but who had put the Black Cats ahead in the game?
**Fabio Borini**

11) Sunderland had knocked Manchester United out at the Semi Final Stage in the 2014 League Cup on penalties, who was in goal for Sunderland in the shoot out?

**Vito Mannone**

# First Goals II – Answers

1) Duncan Watmore
   **Norwich City**

2) David Healy
   **Nottingham Forest**

3) Josh Maja
   **Fulham**

4) Fraizer Campbell
   **Birmingham City**

5) Ji Dong-Won
   **Chelsea**

6) Bryan Oviedo
   **Birmingham City**

7) John O'Shea
   **Tottenham Hotspur**

8) James Vaughan
   **Hull City**

9) Steven Fletcher
   **Swansea City**

10) Billy Jones
    **Newcastle United**

11) Luke O'Nien
    **Shrewsbury Town**

12) Fabio Borini
    **Newcastle United**

13) Lynden Gooch
    **Carlisle United**

14) Chris Maguire
    **Scunthorpe United**

Printed in Great Britain
by Amazon

37162398R10036